MAINE POEMS

BY

LEO CONNELLAN

INTRODUCTION BY
SANFORD PHIPPEN

BLACKBERRY BOOKS
NOBLEBORO, MAINE

Acknowledgements

Lobster Fisherman and Maine are from
Provincetown and Other Poems,
Curbstone Press, 1995.

Unsafe Survivor is from
Short Poems, City Poems - 1944-1998,
Hanover Press, 1998.

Cover Painting by Glenn Chadbourne
Cover Photo by Beth Leonard

Book Design by Christopher Smith

ISBN: 0942396 839

Blackberry Books
617 East Neck Road
Nobleboro, ME 04555

Contents

MAINE POEMS
LEO CONNELLAN

Preface

Leo Connellan of Rockland, Maine is a great and important poet; and Maine people should know about him and read his work because much of what is permanent in the soul of Maine is preserved in his poetry.

When I first read Connellan, twenty years ago, I recognized right away the lost world of my own coastal Maine. Here was a soulmate, a brother, and a powerful poet who grew up in working class Downeast the same way I did. Even though I grew up in the Ellsworth-Mount Desert Island area, the life of the people— my own people—was essentially the same as that of the Rockland fishermen, sardine packers, waitresses, and truck drivers that people the poems of Leo Connellan. His poetry excites me, not just because of the truth-telling and the easy identification, but because of the way in which he writes: he's a convivial and garrulous Maine man with a sharp eye and a great sense of humor, swapping jokes and stories with a bunch of pals in a bar, or down on the dock, telling it like it really is with no holds barred, no censorship, no glossing over. But at the same time, his is the voice of the poet who is a master of the tongue. I love Leo's words, the way he expresses himself. He makes me think of my father, uncles, other Maine men who have suddenly found a brilliant way to articulate their innermost thoughts and deepest feelings.

In 1983, the Humanities Division of the University of Tampa published *Festschrift*, a symposium in book form compiled in honor of Connellan upon the occasion of the poet's having won the Shelley Memorial Award. Twenty-three poets and writers, including such well-known ones as Richard Eberhart, William Stafford, Hayden Carruth, and Donald Junkins, were contributors to this volume.

Maine native poet Kendall Merriam, who grew up in Rockland as did Connellan, offered a "Poem for Leo," in which he says:

Rockland is an anti-intellectual town
if you don't play football
or haul lobsters you have to leave

. . .

a town that doesn't love
pimply faced, gangling boys who write po'try
the town that drives them all away
all of my friends are out-of-staters now
Leo is an out-of-stater now
a Maine boy who made good
with no help from Maine
except for the pain he suffered here
he is a great poet no thanks to Rockland . . .

But in part, the greatness of Connellan's Maine poems is indeed thanks to Rockland and the poet's lifelong quarrel with his hometown; Rockland, or "Lime City," as he calls it in his work, provides the haunting subject matter, the bittersweet memories, and the creative rage that enrich his best poems.

As Connellan himself says in his poem "Wawenock":

It is my night for tears.
Pine tree, umbrella for blueberries,
I am gone, forever from Lime City,
vanished as though an Indian never
slid across Chicawaukee Lake
like all night on a match flame . . .

In "Sea Gulls Wait," he writes:

Come sea gulls, come! I am weak now
In this instant of home, like walking
the earth after my time, the town never
loved me, but I have an ache for this place,
forever the pain is there . . .

Throughout his Maine poems there is the theme of loss: the loss of his mother, who died when he was seven; the loss of family and friends; the loss of home; and the loss of Maine, which he left at 19.

In his Foreword to *Death in Lobsterland* (1978), novelist Hubert Selby, Jr. writes: "These poems come from that part of the soul that's eternally longing to come home, no matter what we may believe is waiting for us. There is that insatiable hunger within all of us to know more than we know, to know the secret of leaves and rocks, to know our mother and father, to know ourselves. And we try to know ourselves by looking around us, but this only tells WHERE we are, not WHO we are. These poems are a song to the WHO we are all looking for through the confusion of our own lobsterland."

In 1995, Sue Walker, editor of *Negative Capability* at the University of Alabama, issued another *Festschrift* on Connellan, as part of the magazine, which featured eighteen of Connellan's poems as well as tributes from both Leo's wife Nancy and daughter Amy.

Survival in the Maine of the 1930s and '40s into which Connellan was born and raised depended upon killing: fishing the coastal waters, chopping down the trees, and hunting deer, birds, and other wildlife for food. Life was hard and basic with the majority of people employed in fish factories, saw mills, lumber and paper mills, on thin-soiled farms, on the railroads and boats, wherever they could find work. Rockland was a working man's town; and Connellan writes wonderfully and movingly about survival among the working folk he knew well.

At the opening of his poem "Lobster Claw," he writes:

> Lobster, I will kill you now,
> crouch in your rocks. Pull up
> your bed covers of seaweed.
> Ride the sea's bottom. Move
> out deep in winter. Burrow
> in mud. Hide under
> kelp. I will bait you

to my family's survival
without conscience. My own
life is in the lines hauling you in . . .

And in his long poem "Amelia, Mrs. Brooks of My Old Child-
hood," he writes:

Great lady of Sardines and
earth and blood, of
blueberryin' years, Clam Factory
years who brought up
children without help, a hopeless
drunk husband beating you in
his futility, when the country was smashed . . .

In "By the Blue Sea," another long, unforgettable poem,
Connellan writes about a fisherman whose clothes "always smelled
of gasoline and fish" and of his "Fish Woman," who suffers from
lifelong unrequited love and from being married to a "mean and
furious husband." Fish Woman finally leaves her husband and
five boys to go and live a completely different life in Boston.

To survive in Connellan's Maine one needed a good sense of
humor; and Connellan is deeply, truthfully funny the way Tennes-
see Williams' tragedies are funny, the way Thomas Wolfe's novels
are funny, the way Flannery O'Connor's stories are funny, the way
Mark Twain is funny.

Another of Connellan's themes is escape the way he escaped
from Rockland and Maine; but he also writes about the people
who can't or won't escape. In the poem "In Lobster Night," he
writes about the local guy who works on a boat, hangs around a
bar called "The Passion Pit," gets drunk, has sex with girls in his
car. It begins:

Otto Fishinfolk, he's
everywhere you go.

Home, just off train,
to the house for a quick change

and that joy of first rushing
downtown to see Main Street again.

Otto's there. "In N'York, aincha!"
"Yes, I am." "Like hit? "I miss
home." "Ayuh, I know hit!"
"Well, see you Otto."

But no, "Hey now, you cummin'
with me tonight. We goin' t'git laid."

There's a poem titled "Maine," in which he writes about how
". . . Maine cannot provide for its bright youth," and which con-
cludes:

. . . There are potatoes here, big as beach balls!
Fish, Lobster, Clams, Sardines. If you're from Maine
your heart is here but nothing for you.

Among some of the Maine native people who appear in
Connellan's poetry runs a thread of mean spiritedness that is
learned and a product from over the generations of the bitter,
hardscrabble existence that too many Mainers have had to endure
from the end of the so-called glorious ship-building days of the
19th century through the Depression years of the 1930s and well
into recent times. An ugly bitter residue remains; and it's evident
in the way neighbors and relatives won't help others out. People
in small towns can be anything but nice to one another, snicker-
ing over someone's failure or shortcoming. These types of people
don't do anything themselves, but if someone does manage to do
something, they want that person to fail so they can laugh at him
or her behind their back.

Richard Eberhart has said of Connellan's work: "He writes
from an honesty and force which grapple with the pain of living
and the drug of dreams; his work is harsh, direct, truth-telling . .
. he gives us long poems informed with dark colors, with tragic
awareness." Poet Karl Shapiro has written: "The narrative
strength reminds me of Robinson Jeffers, the other American

ocean poet. There is nothing stagy about the anguish and nothing fake about the force of the lines." And poet Thomas McGrath has said, "Leo Connellan's poems are not for lovers of the genteel, indeed, it would be difficult to find a poet who seems more ferociously intent on forcing upon us the hard news of failure, the failure of age, of the innocence of youthful hope—even (God help us) the failure of that perennial failure, the American dream. There are many fine short poems and they balance out the longer ones, and it is in the longer poems that Connellan shows his greatest power."

Whether Leo is writing about picking blueberries, the ravages of alcoholism, or about being an Irish Catholic in Protestantland, his poetry is full of great energy and life-giving spirit and rich with earthiness and honest passion. He is often raw, harsh, angry, and profane; but so is life. However, there are marvelous whoops to be had amongst the tragedy, pain, and sadness.

William Packard, the former editor of *The New York Quarterly*, which published a number of Connellan poems, wrote the most comprehensive and lengthy appreciation of Connellan in the 1983 *Festschrift*. About Leo the man, he says: ". . . I remember he always gestured a lot with his hands and he had a voice that would go from soft conspiracy whisper to laughing raucous laughter to a crooning lyric lilt as he read his latest poems out loud. I remember he always had such a strong sense of terror in the air, was always in some turmoil, would always be talking about which people were out to get him and what godawful things were about to happen, and then he would suddenly switch off into an ironic HAR DE HAR HAR voice of some seedy con pitchman . . . I wasn't always sure what to make of this powerhouse poet who was such a walking anthology of voices yet through all the voices there was that Yankee nasal Maine twang that betrayed his own origins, and behind all the paranoia fits and all the verbal hyperventilations, real or imagined, any fool could plainly see that Leo Connellan was a great large heart that would not be denied, and anyone who read over his poems could see that here was an enormous talent that was hellbent on finding its form and taking final shape.

In a review of Connellan's *Shatterhouse*, the second book of his acclaimed trilogy *The Clear Blue Lobster-Water Country* (1985), Packard writes about Connellan the poet, comparing him to Allen Ginsberg, Hart Crane, John Steinbeck, and Eugene O'Neill. As Packard says, "*Shatterhouse* is an ode to America, to American literature, to the damned madness of American families, to the quackery of American psychiatric practices, to the eccentricities of American sexuality, to the American bloodstream violence that is all around us always, and it is also an ode to the human mind and to its ability to cure itself of its own worst illnesses. With the writing of *Shatterhouse*, Leo Connellan assumes his place as major poet in America today, probably better, and from now on we'll have to look backward for comparisons, to all those poets and prose writers Connellan was always reminding us of—Walt Whitman and Stephen Crane and Federico Garcia Lorca and Hart Crane and Washington Irving."

In the 1985 spring issue of *The Greenfield Review*, poet Donald Junkins writes of Connellan and Rockland: "At the heart of Leo Connellan's poems is the sea gull's diet, a documentary spirit, and a lyrical narrative voice. No one writes as well about Maine, its coastal punishments and its inland Spartan ways. Downeast life is the material substance of Connellan's poems, and in them the lobster and its industry becomes his double-edged and ironic metaphor, from *Death in Lobsterland* (1978) to the . . . rare trilogy, *The Clear Blue Lobster-Water Country* (1985). Connellan's subjects are daily life in Maine: its herring industry ("a seine around fish in moon black"); its neighbor-deaths ("cuddling his shoulder with the cheek of a healed broken neck"); its earth rottings ("the long sealed tight lips of the town code"); and its agonizing blood ocean ("granite and lime country, lobster, plush berries popping the hills, Maine my Maine of wild rhubarb, sweet spruce and pine trees, dandelion greens pulled fresh out of your front lawns"). Out of his boyhood life in Rockland, Connellan remembers himself into his Maine poems, and his subjects weigh their biographical anchors under the gull metaphors that transcend history and narrative and remembered denial . . . The lobster is both the red and the black in Connellan's verse and no one understands its shifty mobilities better. The jewel of the sea-mine;

the lucre of its lost causes."

In the 1990s, Connellan has returned to Maine almost every year to read and talk at the University of Maine in Orono, Bowdoin College, Bates College, the University of Maine at Farmington, College of the Atlantic, and a number of high schools including Orono, Houlton, and Ellsworth.

At Orono Public Library, teacher and poet Alex McLean introduced Leo once by saying: "With vivid, burnished words he has documented his 'impossibly rare' life. Like Frost, he has had a 'lover's quarrel' with his world, and his life and work are tidal in their coming and going . . . Wallace Stegner once wrote that 'a place is not a place until someone has written a poem about it.' Because of Leo's ardent investment, Rockland is indeed a place, and Maine is more of a place, and the hard green earth is more of a place. His eye focuses on the primary colors and the primary emotions. You won't find mauve, fuchsia, or magenta in these poems; rather, you will be washed in the blue of the sea, the green of the forest, and in a thousand shades of gray."

In 1996, Leo Connellan became the Poet Laureate of Connecticut and in May 1998 at graduation at the University of Maine at Augusta he was awarded an Honorary Doctorate degree.

Poet Constance Hunting, Professor of English at the University of Maine, who has invited Leo to her poetry classes several times and published him in her literary magazine *Puckerbrush Review*, once told me: "One time I was driving through Dover-Foxcroft at early evening and I saw this fireball going through this farmyard and I thought, 'That's Leo!'"

Connellan's latest book, *Short Poems, City Poems, 1944-1998* (1998), carries a back cover quote from poet Robert Creeley, who lives in Waldoboro and who has recently been awarded the Bollingen Prize from Yale. Mr. Creeley writes: "Leo Connellan's integrity has been a measure for his fellow poets for years and years now . . . his perception and care are as ever unique—his heart a persistent refuge for any one of us, in any time, in any place." Such a quote from Creeley conveys an example of the universal high regard that American poets have for Connellan's work.

Speaking for himself, Dr. Leo "fireball" Connellan has written: "Since you insist, I'll say this as some statement about the act of creating. I think the trick of writing is simplicity. The thing to do is to edit. Once the idea is clear, get rid of excess words. Excess words reveal the writer is bluffing behind nothing to say. I don't rush. The poem will be done when it is. But the minute you have to explain it you're writing prose. Since I often attempt long poems, I hope that I can count on argument with one's self giving my work a chance of being poetry, rather than rhetoric. There are two ways we write. Either we are born brilliant or something disturbs us. All good writing is realized by us because of what the writer has written for the reader to fill in."

What the reader fills in with Connellan is truth.

—— Sanford Phippen
Orono, Maine
April 1999

MAINE POEMS

Wawenock

It is my night for tears.
Pine tree, umbrella of blueberries,
I am gone forever from Lime city,
vanished as though an Indian never
slid across Chicawaukee lake
like all night on a match flame.

Your old country road your
back alleys no longer
know me, the boy
who carried ball bearings
through them in the pockets
of his mud crusted knickers
to kiss marbles into the
slush of spring.

The houses that saw me
cut clothes lines in the
dark cowardice of halloween
pretend they did not, and
the Penobscot sea is
cold blue to my middle years.

Sea Gulls Wait

Sea Gulls at their
flush.

To the granite and lime country, lobster,
plush berries popping the hills, Maine,
my Maine of wild rhubarb, sweet spruce
and pine trees, dandelion greens pulled
fresh out of your front lawn.

Maine of agony, Maine of my blood
and flesh in your earth and ocean. Maine,
I love you, green forests, rugged water,
harbors whose beauty has washed
chaos from my thinking all these years
before I sleep.

Left because of love was not understood
because I was not my father's son in the
pride of his heart and my mother gone dead
on me. Left rather than live
penal servitude outdoors, spirit crushed, joy
turned to broken nerves, left, because I am
of the world, not a vicious niche of it.

Sea Gulls on the edge of my mind's lid
since boyhood. I know you. Do not
wait for me. I will never be
your feast and yet you draw me. I am
set for the town but not you.

You draw me like a fascination with disaster,
an appointment I know I must avoid yet in the
subtlety of our chase I may slip after all

into your bills although all the north winds
cannot drive me into your mouths. I cannot see
how I could come to you. But I must
watch you every instant I breathe.

Winds blow drifts of snow scream my dreams
and you were calling Sea Gulls although I was inland
where the snakes of cities might strike asking
me for a match and when I put my hands into
my pockets cut my pancreas in half with a
blade. Death is only as far from us as it wishes.

I took their daughters. It is too much
for mothers, hawks coveting the bull.
There is no forgiveness from the fish wife,
the farm wife, dreaming their little girls
out of fields, off sea drudgery.

The mothers of daughters I took
would themselves like to kill me, Sea Gulls,
themselves, no one else would be allowed
to do it. It is too much that they could
not step in between me and their daughters.

They slept revenge but the opportunity caught them
asleep. How could a boy know of these set traps
and that is how I slipped through unharmed.

A girl I took as a toothpick youth
with all my blood rushed into my telephone pole
looks at me contemptuously because
a man would have taken her without promises
but I was a sneak in her dress.
Mothers and daughters you constantly haunt me and
I am never in your thoughts except when
you see me and would like to kill me.

Women, mothers, bearers of life, I cannot fathom you;
suffers of the pain that arrives us all
and you do not know life.

But here I am again home in your grasp.
Why did I come back! Sea Gulls, gray and
white in your death your hovering striking
darting under sea water for the kills of
the life in oceans yet you were the
hope of land to ships coming in on their knees.

All the Sea Gulls come down
in their odor of seaweed
gray like faces of strokes snapping
fish bellied as infants gobble,
but without innocence and
the town still wolfing.

Let me go from this place! I am
wild violets crushed in their sweaty palms.
No one has changed. We are together again
in the never healed near fatal
atrocity of my youth.

I will rush from this place this town
where night and morning make no difference.
Invalids do well here and Sea Gulls.

I will leave the sadness of houses their paint split
by uncoerced winter. In each other's arms, love
as you and I know it, knifing our thighs
with twenty nails, no, here man takes
his husband's rights from women setting their lips
against the plunge.

Snow falls the smotherer of victims
who always escape, but not far, through

the high blue berries, yes, the corner beer
store, yes, to struggle fish in boats, yes, into
canning factories, breaking their lives into their youth, yes,
men scooped out as the lobster they go after where
Sea Gulls wait, to the grave, yes, snatched quick from
the pocket book of the undertaker and a whole life
shoveled into the earth forever in seconds.

Yet straight, with no crutch, no dulled
days, home flooded me, though it is no
home to me, but danger.

Drunk in Arizona desert there you were Sea Gulls,
perched on a speck of sand. You were screeching
voice in the wheels of freights.

Crawling San Francisco in blind stagger
I thought you had flown down through the
bars of a couple of drunk tanks and
really had me.

Especially when it rained pouring Sea Gulls
come in from violent out to sea storms, there
were a flock of you Sea Gulls on the piers
of the Embarcadero and I thought to myself
they have me this time.

Come Sea Gulls, come! I am weak now
in this instant of home like walking
the earth after my time. The town never
loved me but I have an ache for this place,
forever the pain is there.

So, try me Sea Gulls; shall we strangle each
other? Perhaps on the sea's rim, Vinalhaven,
island of gouged out quarries beyond
rich green Owl's Head trees salt faded

but unbending, suddenly nothing around us,
Sea Gulls, but open ocean and then the island
and beyond, the whole world through the fog:
shall we play with each other there? No?
In Rockland, you would rather dart for me there?
No? Then you are also coward enough to know your
quarry and I must not even have the end
I feel is mind in your throat.

Where does a man like me die? Probably
in a hallway when my heart finally explodes
not in Maine then home, no, not even
where the scent of the fern is your last breath
licking sea salt from your lips with your last tongue.

I came home to where the blood
of my ancestors colors the snow moon, oh
why did I come back!

Origins

Mother, Father told me you were
like an impossible lily
that does not need earth or drink
and lives forever in my mind
without ever wilting.

The whole New England town was with him
perpetuating your image
for my boyhood heart suffered enough losing you
to Forever at age Seven,
dumped from manhood's dawn
into my middle thirties believing
you were beyond my grasp.

Father never once broke the ribbon on
the packaged secret through to the end of his own life
he loved you that much.

Mother, I never saw you clearly
until during a visit home a friend
slipped her tongue through the long sealed
tight lips of the town code.

Unanswered pieces of my whole life
my senses instinct into place
from way back in the dark storage room of my recall.

As for the town, they wanted me to always
see you as an Angel floating where
religions tell me you wait for me.
Always now you will be exactly as Father described you
to me but now I can see you.

Love you far deeper for being no longer vague,
a perfect someone I could never deserve.

One has to feel flesh, now rotted in the earth
which bore and I know loved me.

Now to Father, I know you have already moved close,
coffins burst into each other's arms again,
as you did the night you made me, now
at last wrap your lover to you for always
and keep him whose love and loyalty to you
never faltered.

The only way I can thank Father, Mother,
is I have put away the bottle.

Old Orchard Beach Maine Burned Down

Fire has leveled my baby's toyland.
We are father and child in the same place.
It was my playpen, too, Sea Weed beach
and the sense of salt and sand on
you and sunburn.

Town of Merry-Go-Round and Donkey cart
rides in dark underground tunnels through
the wonders of horror, down a simulated
mine shaft full of ogres that leaped out
at you. Ferris Wheels town of fun. Children
town burned down. Town of glee-filled laughing
youngsters and hideout motels for lovers right
over the beach. Town of people growing old
on their last time around.

Town for me once when I was young, and
I yearn to go back there now. Town a hurricane
ripped apart in my youth, throwing the Merry-Go-
Round I knew in my boyhood like a scaled saucer,
gone, as we took our only child back where I was
once happy, to a Merry-Go-Round in flames when
Old Orchard Beach Maine burned down, from a
heater too near dry wood and the wind was right.
Again all gone but the scent of fresh pine on
the sea's wind.

                              turned back pages in an ancient
black and molded photo album, yellowing snapshots of
a chubby dark-curled boy and an equally chubby
light-curled boy in what were pinafore suits seated
on the sunny sand beside two huge-hatted choker-
dressed women . . . Aunt Annie and Mamma with the

spindly O O Pier poles and Casino in back, around 1916,
Jim Moore of Glen Cove, Maine, remembers and writes this poet,
. . . in another photo, dad, shirt sleeves rolled up onto
elastics and pant legs rolled to the knees, barefooted with
us boys . . . and in a brown-covered, less molded book, some
earlier Jim Moore girl friends who got waitress and
Chamber jobs at some of the inns, with the same pier in back,
while still later, yes, a couple more blondy beaned boys looking
at the wonders of the old steam peanut machine engine and
cart at the inboard end of the Pier . . . Moore's own kids . . .

What child imagines his own child!
I remember walking these streets, a
boy with no idea that flesh I helped make
would one day love this place too and
be visible in front of my eyes on my memory
back when once I ran ragged swam this sea by
Googins rocks until bleary-eyed exhausted in
happiness, I could no more, but only sleep.

                              dancing out on the pier that fell down.
the old pier with its underpinnings
crammed into sand for fifty years
holding up the ballroom where the
big bands played out over the ocean.

                    There was a luncheonette on the
                    corner of East Grand Avenue that
                    served big thick mayonnaise pickle
                    crab-meat sandwiches squirting out
                    the side of the bread.

                    And perfect rainy movie days,
                    a swim in the warm sea with rain
                    falling on you and dry feeling smooth
                    as a pearl from the ocean swim, into
                    see Brian Donlevy playing "Heliotrope
                    Harry."

Gone, it's all gone, the town's still there, there
is a beach and ocean still, but it belongs to someone
else, the French Canadians, starving for a sea,
Old Orchard Beach Maine is gone for my
daughter too, at six she looked at me, at
only six and said out of her mouth
—"It will never be the same," yes, a six-
year-old said that, she meant they rebuilt
but not the fun games she loved, and she
knew it at only age six, they're gone, all
but the ocean, it's all changed but the
never-ending sea-pounding ocean in Old
Orchard Beach Maine, like a woman you loved
once and can't give up because she's old
and ruined, run down and lived in, but
it will never be the same with her any more,
however you look at her and love comes
back to you . . . love for her, you loved
her once, you couldn't catch your breath for her.

Tell Her That I Fell

Woke me retching and alone.
Within doom booze
her arms around me again
in wished-for honeymoon time
that never happened.

Wait now to become ashes
and am so sorry.

Stagger now, shaking for what I'm running on.
But it takes a few to get started these days,
face gouged by razor unable fingers hold
and each step away from where a bar is near
makes me feel certain I'm going to drop dead.

Each morning now is terror.
The bathroom mirror reflects
earthworms have not a long wait
to pick me clean.
My toothpaste mouthwash
is a breakfast of liquor,
so is all day and every complete night.

Took her once in the snow
the seacoast near, vivid
like if bright red blood was blue.

Afterward when she stood up
the bare spot we melted
was like two halves of a pear.
I know she is in a Fishing Village now
with many babies.
The boats go out each morning before sunup

breaks through salt fog and come in long after dark,
just to make ends meet.

Maybe he is good to her
in his clumsy understanding
I hope so, but never sure in his mind.
Furiously suspicious at any man's glance at her
eternally looking for whoever I am
directly into the face of each tourist who comes
into town.

How it frustrates him, unable
to find and strangle me
who is always the wedge between his best effort,
and he is so strong, sea life hardened.

Wake me these days retching then, all right
just tell her that I fell.
My happiness time was with her,
been any kind of a man
I would have carried her like
a knapsack away and felt
her feet slapping my thighs.

Come on, death, I fear
to wobble the few steps to you.

Fair Warning

Down the dark Pine green,
in deep blue quiet, the
flippers of sea waves
slapping inches off the shore.
Scent of deer moss and fern
soured, all the silence shattered
by the abrupt dog bark of gun blast
rapping the knuckles of water
that let a stranger's boat lie bobbing
and the foreigner lobstering!

Take my virgin daughter if
I don't kick your teeth out,
take my worn out woman
skinny on my provision,
but threaten our living, thief
in my salt flowing refrigerator,
I'll take your life.

Lobster Claw

I

Morning and I
must kill.

Rise in one-bulb light, trying
to move quietly through
thin asbestos-braced house
shuddering at each of my steps,
the one-bulb light crashing
black dying night to
cowardly dawn, ashen at
our endeavor, so quiet
a twig snap jolts me,
as unwelcome surprise to all murderers.

Lobster, I will kill you now,
crouch in your rocks. Pull up
your bed covers of seaweed.
Ride the sea's bottom. Move
out deep in winter. Burrow
in mud. Hide under
kelp. I will bait you
to my family's survival
without conscience. My own
life is in the lines hauling you in.

The sea will rage to
upset my boat and have
you grabbing me in your
right crusher claw into
your efficient stomach
grinding up Mollusks, Algae,

33

and each other. But I
am a survived victim of
old storms. The ocean shrugs
at my approach.

I go, tired, braced
for you by determined
necessity, hope in me
that I can keep my
children from having to
laden their tables
by slaughter, fearing
I never can.

Lobster, let us
get this done. God
you must want me to
do this. Perhaps
the ocean with all its
bluff is not big enough
to keep all you lobster.

I will lay out a string of
redfish-baited traps you
cannot resist.

II

I am an old timer and
give my whole days.
Youngsters no longer
work the long hours, they
come in off the water early
and go to watch rooster-crowing
contests, fight and drink.

The sea is a womb, frothy
like blushing lovers are
shy, but within her,
after all, are the lives
of her many children
killing among themselves,
and she strikes down hard
those too naive to learn
that she is a sea not to be taken.

I am not easily caught,
but overwhelming fatigue
is my nemesis.

III

It is over, men like me
out in boats in the
great sea days. Airplanes
spot you now, lobster, scuba-divers
pluck you taking away your
choice to stay hidden
in ocean bosom or
try to outwit the trap and
win the bait.

We were a breed of men
who could keep such
generated strength in our
sinews and wills as to
break the back of a bear
on a handful of food a
day and walk a hundred
miles, only our
open wilderness is the sea

with hoop net pots
made from iron tires
before Parlor traps, Double
Headers, long gaffing from
small boats on our
bleached-out green rock
coast in blizzard winters,
endless fog summer days
dug into your bones and
never lets go a grip
that inner endurance must be
forged by us to survive,
until, as cow punchers
too long from women we
come in off our water
for fertility ritual and
blood.

IV

Saturday night is
always our time. On the
sea we think of
our women, but mixed
in is the blood of good fights.

Nothing drives a man so
half out of his head as
work that never is enough
for his women and
children, never able
to give your woman
pretty things, your
youngsters something
better than lobstering,
our wind-burned lives
turned old, desperate.

Looking at our thin
frame houses, our pinched
women and our sons
will be out on the
boats with us soon, our
girls rushed to
the first men who
will support them,
whether there is love.

So, the boats in, tied
to their docks, an
edge of ice on the
evening wind, traps
piled to dry on
the wharves, we
walk by tourists come
to Clem's Pound,
picking their dinners
alive out of the day's
haul, frantic in
tanked salt water.
Home, our women
know there is no
stopping us, not
pouring all the liquor
their Baptist hearts
detest will mull
us from this
relished night.

V

There is a dance over to
South Thomaston, Postmaster's
son there from New York wearing

the city clothes of a
man who looks like
he never worked and
Woberton Edgecomb
walked over ready
to break his face
like hitting a glass
lampshade quick,
pulling your hand
back so fast you
don't skin a knuckle,
but the face
goes apart like
it never existed.

But they were talking
instead of going
at it, not
throwing a blow, him,
Postmaster's son
speaking soft, unriled
and damned if
he didn't reach out
and shake Woberton's
hand talking about
how they were through
high school together,
asking Woberton how
he'd been.

That was it! Out on
the sea, the ocean
sure don't ask you or
Clem paying us
grudgingly for our
lobster, but
Postmaster's son

was a Maine boy and
knew us, our
self-contained resentment.

But this here was
our Saturday
night to break heads,
ravish women for our
helplessness, our lives
always on the sea floating
and just then Elmer Tippett
come into South Thomaston
dance hall from Saint George,
the foreigner from
Houlton who'd married
his sister with him. None
of us liked the idea of
his having the little
Tippett girl. Houlton's
Potato country and we're
Lobstermen.
I know the pine trees shook
in their roots when
Woberton Edgecomb turned
his punch meant for
Postmaster's son
and hit the Potato farmer
up off South Thomaston
dance floor like a
barn door struck by
a tractor.
But potato fellas
can hit too, that's
the fun of it!

The getting the sea
and futility out

of you Saturday night
while your women wait
in thin frame houses
wondering how much
of you will have
to be put back together.

That Potato fella
was up at Woberton
and they were
spraying each other's
blood for their years.

I looked to take on
Postmaster's son
come visiting our hell,
then to go back
to his soft city life, the tourists
at Clem's Pound taking their
time selecting our
days' haul like cannibals
over their ruined prisoners,
turned me to murderous
hatred and right then
Postmaster's son would
have gone home in a
basket of my aggravation, even
if he did ask Woberton
how he was, but
Postmaster's son
was gone, using
the kind of brains
that escaped him from
the boats everyday life,
come home one time finally
busted apart, either
by a Saturday night

fight, Southern Comfort
full up back seat
auto fornication, or
the sea at last
too much to take on.

VI

Lobster, colored
blue green, sky blue,
bright red, and even
albino, I'll find you.

I string my baited traps
each dawn and come after
them in the afternoon, and
the later I come back the
more of you lobster are
in them.

If you're "shorts," too small,
I throw you back, cursing
my waiting, my labor
for a lobster like you,
not big enough to bring
in and sell.

In the whole seas of
the world, Rockland, Maine,
is your home, lobster,
vulnerable shedding
your shell, helpless
as larvae floating
the ocean and later,
weak of your many

joints, claws, your
body easily snapped.

No one ever forgets the
sweet taste of lobster
claw meat driftwood
fire cooked beneath
steaming heaps of seaweed.

I must go out through
thick early morning
fog until sun burns
it off and I can
see. It is in this
darkness and then the
black of evening, when
I wearily ache, that I
could go wrong. So,
Morning I watch you,
and Evening, my eyes
are on you from noon.

Something I
did not consider, flame
near the boat's gas tank
could take me, and
it was the last thing
on my mind when
the blast threw me a
half mile all cut up
in pieces for you, lobster.

VII

I'd rather finish
spitting at sea spray
that has slapped my

face fifty years,
than in some chair, but
my woman has spent
our lives waiting for
sundown when I
come into her arms.
Ocean, I owe her
some time and
Lobster you shall
not deny her.

No, Lobster, you shall
not have me. My
woman would like
to see once again
what I look like in
daylight for awhile
before we are no more
than the faces of clouds.

And all the heavy rain
down on lobsterman already
fighting the water that
is ocean, is our tears
weeping for knowledge
of him.

It is the sea mother
who whips him in a
wrath of wind like a
snarling cornered cat
while lobstermen
rip out her children.

So, to it then and
a day on the sea, fresh
wind and salt free
feeling. Tossing

the bowed trap, whichever
you think takes
strain best and I
take my chances on borers,
rather than risk
termite-treating
the traps and lose the
haul.

Morning again, and I must kill
to exist. Lobster,
scavenger crustacean,
why should I so mind
killing you!

Maine

Here is dark blood green rich blue.
Sea Gulls, big bulbous freckled
red strawberries, blackberries burst
their bushes. Cold winter forces our
using ourselves. Summer will burn us
with its sun and run. Autumn hauls
bright Fall to brown dust. The sea
changes its colors at whim yet can
hit beaches furious, drawing back to strike.
The human here is lost in survival isolation.
Gnawing, always feeling we've left out something
we cannot define. Hunger is narrow irritability
with no time to philosophize in the sun baking
cold attitude that draws sighs of erotic delight
from tourists but ignores, betrays, kills its own; makes
us feel, though Maine cannot provide for its bright youth,
that we need an invisible passport if we leave, to
come back. There are potatoes here, big as beach balls!
Fish, Lobster, Clams, Sardines. If you're from Maine
your heart is here but nothing for you.

Lobster Fisherman

It's May-n-we gut th'lobster fever agin,
th'cold sea splashed freedom of hit but
computers make catchin' lobster such a
sure thing bringinin too many s'that
price drops and 's' not worth hit.
Once we had only a piece of rope and a weight
to find a ledge in th'sea leadin' from
shallow to deep water lobster come
to shed their shells so they can grow bigger
into our traps. now anyone-n-everyone
with instruments that register depth and
ocean floor, technology takin' too much
until now th'thrill for doin' hit in wind
sea salt sand anticipation vanish.
Th'scavengers are saved by scavengers.

By the Blue Sea

She used to walk by
the house of the boy she
loved hoping he'd see her
and come out.

Slowly she walked by, love
a spike in her wind pipe . . . dry
throat ache and pain all
she got for loving the boy
who took her by the blue sea

but would not come out
of his house and take her
inside to keep

       He had no job or money, he
       wasn't supposed to be
       doing what they were doing.

He liked the love making
near rocks that jagged
up through flesh skinning sand,
but there was no way he could
come out of his house to her
when she walked slowly by.

Finally, she took a man who
had the same job the
father of the boy she
wanted had and so there!
But she didn't have him.
And her husband went
out every night, not with

women or to drink but
out on a boat, a Dragger, out in
dark ocean.

He was a mean husband and
furious. He bent the prongs
of a fork to show his
evil strength to her if
she crossed him, like by
bearing a daughter.

She bore him five sons
in six years, five sons
and only wanted him to
come home to her evenings
from his fine job as good
as the job the father of
the boy she loved and
couldn't have had.

But her husband didn't
see a woman telling him
how to live and went out
of Harbor, Maine on a
Dragger after Sardines,
Mackerel . . .

    He's had what he wants of
    you Fish Woman so he goes
    out on a boat after
    other helpless things leaving
    you alone in pitch quiet, alone,
    his love is the fish lust of your carcass,
    and the stalking cowardice of illiterates
    who prey on fish who can't get away
    through slippery water . . .

He liked being out on
the ocean with no people
coming in you got to wait on.

His clothes always smelled
of gasoline and fish.

And with his perpetual
dead cigar he always`
smelled from combination
cigar fish and gasoline like
the smell from first touch
of a match to fresh cigarette
making young children
car sick . . . he
was something to wait for
to crawl into bed with.

Well, all this time the
boy Fish Woman loved back
by the sea where Burdock
bushes stuck in his hair
like shot Porcupine quills,
boy she loved had failed
the pretentious pisspot aristocracy
expectations of his family
and those years from
time to time would stagger
in and out of countries and states
full of Molson of Canada or the
Ballantine of New York and
one evening in the dark
parking lot of a Damariscotta
dance hall he staggered up to her
and still even then to her
he was still even then one
of those lovely people she had

hoped to marry into and she
knew if he ever stepped
inside dance hall that night,
her husband, breaking ritual
and taking her dancing that night, hoping
to cure all this foolishness 'bout
his being home with her nights, her
husband would lay his eyes on
the boy she really loved and
at last have him victim
for all her imagined coldness
to him, now her husband would
beat the boy she loved into
hospital or dead and
that night under the
singing leaves of lust in a
dance hall parking lot Fish
Woman protecting mother of
staggering boy of the blue pines.

There in the cold moonlight
thinking thoughts like how
he could get her again, he actually
stood there and asked her if
she'd still go with him even now
if he finally came to her.

He babbled he'd take
her five children too . . . her and
her five children . . . She looked at
him sadly and smiled and said
she would, standing there knowing
he never would come for her but now
she knew it was because he was
a breathing dead man.

She never expected to
see him again where the

Pines came down there
ringing them in an
embrace of doom.

Well, she was a proud girl,
too alive to allow herself
to die in an empty house
where the man went
chugging out to sea nights.

Her beauty was English, the
Falcon nose, but
poverty showed in her set mouth.

And she had the guts
of women who stood
on Widow walks knowing
their men dead out through
the salt splashing fog.

And she left her sons
to save herself.
She tore herself from
her children to survive.

The way life was put to her
she has a right to, if she
could do it . . . leave her children . . .

>   I hear the crying
>   children at the
>   loss of their mother . . . little
>   things sitting looking out
>   windows at anything that moved,
>   the wind, trees
>   swishing and swaying
>   expecting it was mama

come home, but
she never came.

The way her life was she
had to tell herself that
a woman wouldn't know
what boys need to know . . .

It was a hard thing to do
leave her sons, I do not
judge lest someone see
me for what I really am, see!

Fish Husband who had the
same job as the father of
the boy she loved whose
house she used to walk
slowly by, Fish Husband
could go out off
on the sea and that
was alright . . .

But for her to want anything
the least of which was to
simply have him home with
her in the dreary house at night
was supposed to be more
than her right.

And it was the usual
sorrow back and forth.

You cannot make children
with someone and leave
just like that!

Back and forth, she

tried it again with the
man who had the same
job as the father of the
boy she loved, but once
something is broken it
is destroyed . . .

      and children are destroyed
      crying children, her
      heart broken boys sitting
      looking out windows
      thinking since she
      came back once she'd come
      back again, but she didn't.

Once again she struck out
into the world of jibes, world
of hatred for people who
do not just accept their death.

Finally, again, she married
(you have to eat), a man who
was so happy to have her he
bowed to everyone in church
as they got married.

And Fish Husband she left, no
sooner she was gone, took
another woman to wipe
noses, clean and
cook for a flock, who
didn't mind his saddling
up and riding the
range of the sea, she had her
Charlie Pride records, who
soon presented him with
a little girl who completely took

over his heart, he was wild about
her, he, who had bent fork prongs and
shoving them under the nose of
Fish Woman Lurleen who used to
walk slowly in front of the
house of the boy she loved who
didn't come out to her . . .

        Her boys grew up to
        tell her how as children
        they'd indicate their
        father's second woman
        as their mother, ashamed
        to tell anyone their real
        mother was alive divorced living
        up in Boston . . . They didn't know
        how to tell anyone
        their real mother wasn't dead
        for leaving them.

Now, another life later, the
boy in some need, survived and
lived long enough to throw her
on her back again and climb on,
whatever, maybe just to find her to
erase those things that horrify our memory, now
one day the boy she loved all those years ago
by the blue sea . . . now

one day the boy she
loved all those years ago
came to see what he could
get or regret but her
second husband was fresh cold
and going with him wouldn't
look right, besides love is
hatred when used or ignored.

. . . "I loved you once"
she told him now without feeling,
she told him from way deep inside like
there was a little her inside herself
calling from long ago . . . "I loved you once."

Calling "I loved you once" now
to him like retreating
surf of ocean spraying as
waves come in from way back deep.
Her face did not move
and it was a voice
of love that had died walking
past his house hoping he'd
come out, that said to
him now . . . "no more, no more, but . . . I loved you once."

Now when he looked up at her,
she putting horror in
him, sinking feeling, she told
him he picked a day to
find her, her
second husband who bent
over at the middle so
glad was he to get her,
dropped dead and that
his coming now made her
feel that the sudden
massive coronary death
of her second husband must
be punishment for her

      leaving her children, for
the times he and she they
lay under pines by
the blue sea . . .

She told him she
used to lie pregnant
fearing the babies
would come out with
three heads because
of what he and she
did by the pines
near blue ocean all those
years ago, even in snow, by

the blue sea frosting
each other's eyes with our breaths.

In Lobster Night

I

Otto Fishinfolk, he's
everywhere you go. '

Home, just off train,
to the house for a quick change
and that joy of first rushing
downtown to see Main street again.

Otto's there. "In N'York, aincha!"
"Yes, I am." "Like hit?" "I miss
home." "Ayuh, I know hit!"
"Well, see you Otto."

But no, "Hey now, you cummin'
with me tonight. We goin't'git laid."

You fear if you say no, the horror
of something you cannot conceive.

He can smell your fear of his violence
if you don't come and makes you go
with him stalking a night of lust.

In dark green
of the Lobster town.

Unable perhaps to face
really wishing to flutter.
He needs you violated, your
life happiness spoiled.

Devoured, you rush away from home
and forever the beauty is all dirty.

You come home drawn back by
need to come from some place
even after you got away.

The wild furious ocean never
said you could leave, the sea
like wrinkles in a turtle's neck
calls you back.

You come home and can't get away
from Otto, he's overwhelming, others
observing you two would resent you
with disgust that you don't stand up
for yourself, say no to Otto, that
you won't go with him.

But then he'd come after you
in a carfull of Ottos out of Port Clyde
to explode the boredom.

And you can't simply say
"Otto, I don't get home all
that often, have places, people
to see and spend time with my
father because our time together
is gone." The light in his winter
eyes is fading.

II

We were after the Kaylor sisters,
Otto parked and into Del's Pool Room,
cold cigar smell in spittoons, smoke

on pool table green.
Charlie Tyler playing points when
we come in, there was a thing 'bout
Leatrice Butler between Otto and Charlie, she
come to Saturday night good time with clear
understanding she leavin' with Otto once
"Four Haddocks And A Hake," his group finished
up with "Granddad's In Thomaston Wishin' He
Wusn't," but when Otto come to take her she'd
snuck out with Charlie . . . what Otto wanted me
along now to see or do I didn't know, I was in
the horror of terror. Without seeming to move
Charlie slammed Otto on the forehead
with the back of his pool cue without
even turning or seeming to miss the rhythm
of his shot. Otto almost went down but he
didn't and the shoeshine air was full of death.

It screamed out of pool room silence
and was in everybody's champing hesitation
like lobster blood might get out of human skin.

My breath clotted
in the fury.

But it suddenly passed as though pre-arranged,
Otto said to Charlie Tyler 'I'll be wanderin'
-n-you know Leatrice Butler's mine to pass out
not yours to take, wimmin is special, still, when
I cum where you are, whallop me agoodun as I'd do by
you by Gawd when you're fed up with the sea of blueberryin'.

And so out of Del's on this horror, because Otto
had to have me know he could take anything he wanted
in Penobscot without leaving, who did I think I
was to leave . . . you can be Postmaster's son or Kelsey
Fishinfolk's boy, but you're an outsider forever

because you left, evidently thought you were
better-n-everybody.

In dark bar called by every yearning boy "The
Passion Pit," blueberry pickers with fishingmen
off boats and Sardine people with the crumpled
green of their hard work going in two drinks of
a shot glass to twangs of Otto heading "Four
Haddocks And A Hake," possibly rendering "High Holin'
In Th'Blueberries" . . . he vents himself on victims
who yearn for his excitement in this dull place.

III

In the blood night of chaotic poverty
Otto took me to get the Kaylor sisters
in Union, to drive some place full
of pine and balsam smell in mosquito
heat and plunge into.

When we came into their home the lobster
moon turned orange, the parents looked
away as though they couldn't offer
much life to the girls and even if the
bible told them Otto was the devil, still,
if they wanted the sight of their children,
if they didn't want them to go die on the
lower East Side, or in the waters of
San Diego, they'd better say nothing.

The lust in me wanted their daughter
but my eyes could not look at them.
Strange, the sneak in my nature tried
to make believe now, to make it a
secret from the real me that I was
erotic and wanted her. The earth

in me wanted the girl, while I would
have protested in horror the rape.
The girls knew why we had come for
them and what they were heading to do
if they wanted Otto Fishinfolk and the
only excitement around Penobscot town
week-end nights when he stands center
at "The Pit" bludgeoning the world
with a guitar.

IV

We drove into green woods. The lobster
were shedding their claws. Little mosquitoes
hovered over our sweat and had us like
over ripe fruit. In the woods, in dead
green, the dull dark green Maine winter
does to green, and murdered lobster
thrashing their lives out in the traps
of the bay does to green, taking the
bright life from the land that
allows death in the sea.

Otto stopped the car and said over his
shoulder to Rita Kaylor, "You takin'"
and she nodded, but it was his orders
she took, not me.

Already her sister Elvira Kaylor was
undressed naked and sobbing for Otto
who crawled on her chewing on a toothpick
while under me Rita was like a run away
plumber's snake, with her eyes closed, but
I didn't feet I was the lover she was
moaning to in lobster night.

But we were too big for the car, four
of us churning butter so I climbed
over her and was gone in the black.
She rushed out too, it was so good that
suddenly I loved Otto, a great surge
of the joy in hot lust, outside by the lake
I put her on the ground and she tickled
the sky with her toes while I extinguished
myself. Crushed rock sand cut my knee caps.
Cricket churp went quiet. Slippery sweat itched.
Suddenly a quiet fury in the used girls.
We were all stifled in sour let down.
It was awful by the lake now. There was no
wake for the death of ourselves.

Shadows

I cannot look at birds or hear
them singing. We failed
to be men in the flood of our youth,
how can we ever be old men!
We will be shadows, shells
of carcasses rocking on porches
until the wind explodes us
and we are the foul smell
in the air turning the noses
of lovers and children, in
some vague future peace time.
I have nodded to God and
He looked right through me.

A Witness

Sea Gulls beating wings
I saw you dying.
The sun turned its back
and I was driving
when you fluttered on the sidewalk.

Come in close from twenty straight days of rain
over the cruel ocean
to seek food where storms dump our refuse
open for the picking;
flew into a wall you did not understand
that springs on all of us
who might have won
alone and unsurrounded, fighting,
if we knew what was to be beaten.

Closed Wake

Silence, I am seeking quiet.
My insides no longer burst to flowers
or hay like the smell of sun
on the back of your hand.

My foot smacked rivers,
and I paddled canoes on pure water,
before defecating boats, until
animals would not some to drink.

We packed our bags for a planet,
leaving only tombstones.

After exhausting calcareous tissue
of all the slaughter, we dug Indians up,
shipping their bones to make buttons.
Now computers stalk us.

I love the woods. All the
wilderness is come down.
We are in cages of mortar.
Our open plains become skid rows
of the flood tide of penises
until cactus needles wilt.
If we had only used our brains instead.

Penobscot Raccoons

Rushing raccoon sound
in Higganum wood.

And far off in Glen Cove,
Maine, raccoon rushing
sound through Jim Moore's
window in emphysema death
sound oceans make.

      Sea Gulls fast down
after sardines along the
wharves of the town. Herring
is vile odor on the blue.

In long sheds of Sardine factories
men push racks of thin rusted
scaly trays called flakes because
dead sardines lay on them and stick
in the hot ovens; human beings
rise early, long before cold black dark
is stabbed by orange morning and come
to earn their food pushing the loaded
flakes into big ovens in heat, men like
raccoons scurrying, rushing from the
heat, pushing the loaded flakes in to cook,
in and out, into heat and out all day
after women sitting across the conveyer
belt slice off herring heads and tails
and are paid for the speed they
can load up racks of the flake trays.
The fish do not know it, their
life strangled from them forced

into oxygen. What we live on kills
another as our head under the water
of their world kills us . . . death no
surprise to Jim Moore . . . death always
part of Jim as all newspapermen
fill rag paper with the ruthless cold
print of the man who drove
eighty miles an hour on
Rockland, Maine's Old Country Road
and dumped himself and
three children into a
bottomless quarry.

Then raccoons were
frantic in air bubbles . . .

In Higganum, Connecticut wood,
the sound raccoons make
rushing through houses
and flames of fire make
crackling on dry wood.

And screams as
the sea screams
through Jim Moore's window,
always the splashing sea, Jim
knew in that alert haunting instinct
which causes the intuitive to
sense death in serenity
that there is no earthly
happiness but only time
survival struggling
for just a touch of love.
But who lives
as if this is so, in
Higganum wood the
man's grandchildren . . .

Sudden rushing of
raccoons sounding through
my ears . . . glass shattering
tinkling death sound far off
in quiet Higganum wood.

Fire, everyone trying to
save on oil, old fashioned
wood stove without
old fashioned experience.
Fire squeezing like
white past from hot
old wood stove pipe lying
like a tongue on an icicle
rips flesh, flame
burst the baseboard.

In Higganum wood
the man's grandchildren
died but if it wasn't
an old wood stove with
its pipe too close
to dried wood of the house
you would have gone in
a hundred years anyway
or forty but I your
grandfather would not
have had to wake up from
my bed and there was the
Penobscot sea again like
raccoons rushing in my
ears and across orange lit
darkness in December cold
with the Christ child only
mangers away, children
trapped scurrying like
raccoons in an attic of flames.

Raccoons with
the ocean in my
filled head, Penobscot
raccoons in
Higganum wood, glass
tinkling and your screams
while fire tried
to burn down the sky.

And across the haze
of my eyes you died . . . I
should have been gone, not you.
Your grandmother should have
been gone, not you, by
right we'd all be dead
before you, your mother's
breasts would not forever have
a stake of pain heavy between them
from aching for you, we'd
have been lucky enough to be gone
before you, but God has decided
that we must see you go
before we do, this is Hell.

Your father took
an ax to the old
wood stove because
something had to be gone after.

Scott Huff

Think tonight of sixteen
year old Scott Huff of
Maine driving home fell asleep at
the wheel, his car sprang awake
from the weight of h is foot head on
into a tree. God, if you need him
take him asking me to believe in
you because there are yellow buttercups,
salmon for my heart in the rivers,.
fresh springs of ice cold water running away.
You can have all these back for Scott Huff.

Edwin Coombs

Edwin Coombs is dead.
I just saw him.

And I talked to him on the telephone.
But he's dead.

I see Edwin fresh home from
the Marines, the Second
World War over and I'll be
getting out of Rockland, Maine
High School soon. We've got a
lot to talk about, plans to
make . . . he's dead!

In anguish I think everything,
imagine him murdered!

What occurred!? Undoubtedly nothing
but freak tragedy fluke of circumstance
and it is my broken heart reacting.

What happened!
What does "Falling in love" mean?
Marrying Betty Grable face, Jane Fonda
backside, Jane Russell breasts, but
not a person.

Our life for fantasy people
willing to put out for another
victim, shall we
make my boyhood friend's
death, murder?

I could say in my grief that
his wives murdered him, the
first one, say, not living
long enough to accomplish his
death, he, unaware she
wanted him dead but after
a long time at her pleasure,
he, unknowingly proceeding
to choose the woman who would
be his widow to marry, but why
would she kill him, why should she,
how! . . . By needling him? . . . until
finally exasperated he
sprang to death, not suicide
but self death of anyone marrying
face and body but not the
person who "realized"
it, that they were
loved for what they looked like,
not themselves, perhaps
unconsciously, but more
likely cold bloodedly exactly
retaliating for that awful
kind of feeling being used as
a lust receptacle rejected
visualizing ourselves as
loved frantically, sweaty
loved, jerked in, like a
bicycle Tire Pump is loved,
petted, fondled by the sweaty
anticipating hand while
it fills up the wheels making
possible ego satisfying rides
even as he ejaculates in you
with his eyes closed so you
never know who he's dreaming
of as the hot splattering of

loads rests him on you a
hulk ready to snore which
would be alright if you knew
he loved you but what he loves,
if indeed he loves at all, is
your Betty Grable face, Jane
Fonda backside, Jane Russell
breasts . . . he never conceives
you're onto his fantasies and
out for vengeance in your
disgust so is bewildered
as to why being with you
is no longer fun but deadly.

He does not comprehend
it is deadly until he
is dead, then, up floating
over himself he knows, but
like a balloon the air
is let out of he's
swishing off into the gone.

None of us ever saw
much of Edwin after
he married.

He trusted that woman
for something he thought she'd
"see" he needed and give
him, he wasn't self sufficient
and she broke him and he
liked it. It hurt and was
warm, violent and sensual
and that first wife helped
him fail which he couldn't
stop himself from needing.

I had not seen Edwin
for a couple of years ever
since the small difference
of age between us was
caught up and I had been
away in a uniform too, back,
I stopped by his married home.
It was foreboding, dark,
bleak and he met me shuffling,
taking the tack that I was
still young, single, wouldn't
know the new rule of living
on a man when he gets married.
But we had been very close
so he couldn't bring himself
not to take me into the house
and introduce me to the woman.
She was a quiet one, absolutely
physically beautiful
in an olive way and cold.
However I could see making
love to that face, that
mouth, that body and she
saw I could, suddenly
smiling that such lust
was possible for my life.

I know Edwin saw clearly
the bargain we might be
striking but he slunk
out of the way turned
not to interfere. This
was all part of the
warm hurt violent and
sensual she inflicted
on him as part of their
relationship which he

liked like children·with
freshly spanked bottoms
often seem to need to
throw their arms around
their beaters as though
for agreement, reassurance,
they've been hit and now it's
over and they can at least
count on the relationship . . .
What did she have that held
him, something! He stayed
with her twenty years until
she died . . . She had
planned him dead but
his luck was her death.
Perhaps it was his
Yankee New England
morality or guilt that
held him with her but
more like need, she was
punishment, something he
needed.

She was a quiet one, dark of
mood, cold, vicious. Edwin's
friends never saw him about
after she got him, once he
married that woman, no,
never in Del's Pool Room
anymore or in "The Passion
Pit" with the boys drinking
with a girl from Saint George
or from Hope, a big cigar
in his teeth, his head in
a stetson biting the
big cigar, grinning,
talking hard, ready to fight

enjoying the feel of the open
hand slapping someone
and the head clearing slap back.
I used to be hanging along
in the shadow of legendary Edwin
waiting for his hard guy type
of remark through clenched
teeth and follow him with a
crowd of the boys up into
hotel room for fun with
Fish Women from over to
South Warren; once they were
all spread out on the floor
Southern Comfort full and
I was the only one who could
move, so later Elvira Camiston
from down th' harbor told Edwin
. . . "That young-un with th' ears
he's goo-ud! Bring him next
time, Edwin, he c'n pump
like hell-n-cum off too!"

. . . Realize Edwin's widow
as the kind of woman he
needed . . . no matter what
egged him Edwin got up out
of that Sunday afternoon
chair all by himself
and dashed out to death.
No other's arms forcibly
lifted him nor was he
dragged by force . . . what
gave way in him, what
blocked his comprehension
like a Pittsburgh steel
worker climbing right into
blast furnace roaring flames he

reaches cold steel in to melt
the only time iron weeps.

. . . Some survive by devouring,
but then he chose women for
what he wanted from them and
would rather have it than his life.

He wouldn't admit that but he
cautioned me no four letter
words or any remarks that
would mean she wouldn't
let me come again. Edwin,
a grown man of 53 said that
to me.

In his home, when we met
after years, after a long time
Edwin showed me two hundred
year old rooms and told me
plans that sound like he
didn't need her, the way
youth, boys will talk about
camping and fishing, outdoor
hunting trips without thought
of a girl in them and when
woman is in their lives,
often never talk that way again.

Edwin Coombs said to me the things
he had not done but would do, that
afternoon I saw him once more
once again after a long time.

When I saw him after years
his face was like sifted ashes.

I remember the blond handsome
youth with sensuous lips and
amused self confident strutting.

I remember thinking
as I saw him after a long time
. . . he looks dead, the blood looks
sucked out of his face like his
life raw egg through punctured shell
is going only by a beat.

What is happening here for
my eyes to see if they will!

Probably nothing it is
only my heartbreak . . . still
he looked grey like a man might
look if he thought to himself
in his head he was dead . . . if
the situation of his living
was become so bad, he was
grey like that.

But we know his widow,
no one could ever meet a finer woman.
She is the survivor of three men.

Why should she kill him! She didn't!
I am heart broken and looking for anything
to blame, anyone, my boyhood
friend is gone.

And it is my broken heart falling on
a good woman, no better, no worse
than any of us, lovely, beautiful
to see and assume.

My boyhood friend is dead
and I am full of grief
which for a cold one like me
is forgotten experience.

I remember when I visited
she looked at me sourly,
contemplatively, her lips
clamped down making her
nose look bulbous and
slightly to the left
as if annoyed by the
possibility of the one someone
or something that could
jerk Edwin out of her control.

Coming into the house I sensed
her wondering if she must
match wits with me so I
played simpleton to look
to her incapable of comprehending
and since, luckily, some of us
are so foolish as to think
others do not see us exactly
and clearly and that our life
is the toleration of others,
her eyes took a look at me
and dismissed me and in order
to be with Edwin again, I
threw up the invisible mesh
veil of monopoly conversation
and sure enough she said to
me later . . . "You know, you
took over so, Edwin felt
completely left out. He wanted
to talk too, to show you some things."

But I felt that was better
than for her to feel threatened
by me so I wouldn't be
welcome to come see
Edwin at all anymore.

She, absolutely physically
beautiful, married twice
before she met Edwin, twice
survived little boy chauvinists,
the man she had her children
by had such an accident off a
diving board as to completely
paralyze him for life. He
was alive, could blink his
eyes, talk; somehow her
son, a little child at the
time, was given the burden
of the blame for the man's
diving board accident . . .

. . . as if there wasn't enough
water in the pool to dive into
and it was a small boy's fault!

. . . as if thick ropy weave
diving board was soapy slippery
and it was a small boy's fault!

. . . Who knows how a strong young man
became broken to pieces! But
for the sanity of everyone
she didn't stay around to
carry any bedpans, no, she
married a man she wouldn't
have if she'd see how
infuriated a woman like

her made him, a woman who
abruptly shut him off and took
to her bed loaded on pills
so later no one could ever
demand to know why she didn't
come out and face an issue, he
went into rages when
he "realized" her and
in put him in a mental hospital.

. . . Someone will think
"She's not a very good woman,
didn't stay with the diving board man,"
have human compassion . . . who ever
had any compassion for her!?

Where did her hatred begin!?
. . . if, in fact, she wasn't born
cruel in her nature, if man
created poison in her, when!?
As a little doll on a man's knee
with his fingers feeling up
under her dress . . . Did a
gang of men get her out
in horrible whistling green
of dance hall woods with
Glenn Miller's "Moonlight Serenade"
drowning out her calls for help while
they pumped murder into her.

But where does evil come from?
What could make a beautiful woman
hate so much that she'd allow her
own male son to have his life scarred
feeling he was responsible
for an accident that broke
his father like glass . . .

. . . if she couldn't get the boys
who got her she'd make one to get
and she'd get everyone, every man
she ever could . . . the first thing
she told me she did, that time
I saw Edwin again after a
long time, right after she
married Edwin they went
to a gathering of Antique
Dealers and publicly she
just picked up some antiques
and put them onto the back
of their truck, stole
antiques and put them in
their truck knowing they'd
be kicked out of the Antique
Dealers' Association, but
that was getting Edwin right
from the start, just so he got
in case, apparently, her luck
ran out, something prevented
her usual plan.

I was appalled hearing it, but
more by the way Edwin just
stood there hearing her tell
it to me and laugh like
it was really a smart stunt, he
just stood there and took it, she
was his pin-up girl with
Betty Grable face in a
bathing suit hiding Jane Fonda
backside and those
Jane Russell breasts almost burst
through swimming suit,
lugged around in U.S.
Marine duffel bag and

pinned up on walls . . . when
Edwin saw her it was 1943
again, and the sadness is
he meant her no disrespect,
would like to have loved
her inside as a person but
he didn't understand and
could have died believing
that she "knew" what she
looked like and "was
completely satisfied" that
he loved her face and
figure which had always
been yearned for ever
since she could remember,
lusted after to strains of
Glenn Miller's "Moonlight
Serenade" but after
years of it, even in this
liberated "Ms." feminist
time, she really got to
the point where she almost
wouldn't have minded some
unshaven man saying to
her "Come here, Broad!"
or "if you want to know
where the Public Library in
Bangor, Maine is, Babe, you
get up off your butt,
drive to Bangor and ask
a cop!" It really would
have been a change . . . a
"crude" change, and no one
likes being referred to
as a "Broad," but, still
someone might be talking
to her as flesh and blood

woman instead of as the
last male symbol,
visualized as men wanted
her and she had the
strength and courage to
leave relationships and
push herself above the
male idea, to survive it,
even if that involved a
little smashed death here
and there, a great woman!

Edwin so frail
even as a young man
back from the Marines, he
affected cockiness but
wavered even staggering
in his voice, you
almost expected him to
crumble to dust and vanish.

All us High School boys heard
stories about his legendary
cock prowess, a "must" in those
days to be important in the
Lime town, but I tell you
he was more like the
snapped stem of a tulip
than any steel rod.

He could be moved to
sudden violence and then
kill you with his fists
if you riled his sensibilities.
But if he loved you, you had him.
He would put up with
anything for love, abuse if you
cuddled him after the punishment.

If you were his comrade too
you had him, he could never
conceive you'd harm him.

Who knows what occurred!
It was so impulsive
like people drinking and someone
comes in excitedly yelling
. . . "There's a man over in
your woods helping himself
to a Christmas tree cutting down
one of your Evergreens" . . . and
the way Edwin dashed
out in his car to middle
of main highway and
seemingly oblivious
of the danger, makes
one wonder who needled who
to rush after some
man cutting down a tree . . . was
it worth your life
to stop someone ending
a tree's life?

You know how sundown
sets you up, blood green
of evening dark when
day drops behind a
fan of dusk . . . Edwin
Coombs, my boyhood friend
heard in Christmas time,
man on his land to
cut trees with no
permission and you can't
just have what your eyes takes
so he went outside with his
wife to protect what was theirs
and in that wanton way we

85

go cruising his car slid
along main highway breakdown
lane until he saw the man, and he
leaped out of his car burst
vehemently into middle highway at
night's coming when the
evening sits down on your life.

I can see him as he looked
before death ran him over his
head cocked like he was
cuddling his shoulder with
his cheek of a healed broken neck,
he always looked a broken bird
put together again . . . now
gesturing oblivious of where
he stood as a driver who would
never remember death borrowing him
to steal Edwin in that low twilight
just as dark takes your eyesight;
my boyhood friend become ashes
scattered now somewhere over home.

Amelia, Mrs. Brooks of My Old Childhood

I

Amelia, Mrs. Brooks of my old childhood
I have come to you again.

I was job training in
New Jersey and a letter
came from someone
we did not know.

I asked my wife to
read it to me over
the telephone in
vague, irritated curiosity
and it was from someone
I had never heard of, your
Sister-in-law.

She admonished you loved me so much I
ought to be ashamed at my neglect of you, all these years.

II

       "No-o, Amelyuh duzzent
live withus . . . No-o, Amelyuh's
across th'bridge t'Brewer, in a
nice nursing home . . . a nice! nursing home-n-her boys
live near by . . . No-o, Amelyuh don't know
y'cummin' . . . I wrote you. It was
my idea . . . I'll go telephone her now!
Y'gut a minute haven't you!? You'll go
see her!?"

. . . This one resents! She
can't put her finger on it but there's
something in the loose free easy
way I materialize at her door from
miles away within week of receiving
a letter she just dashed off for
whatever reason . . . or was it
overwhelming for her to write . . . ?

She can't put it
into words but what it is is her kind
has lost control of me. I move in an out
and around them as I please and if I
please . . . I got away . . . she knows
I got away!

From thin foundationless houses
plunked onto the earth, to the left a little from
Maine winters, like the old bow legged ladies inside,
sagging on teacher's pensions and dying in a rut
unable to even take a car trip because gas and motels
cost, stuck in the house for life, the only thing in
their lives now, dragging out to supermarket for
hamburger to make endless never changing meals of
meat cakes, peas, mashed potatoes cold in their pepper and salt
with the never melted butter clinging like a car that
has skidded on ice under snow to the side of a snow bank.

III

Great lady of Sardines and
earth and blood of
Blueberryin' years, Clam Factory
years who brought up
children without help, a hopeless
drunk husband beating you in

his futility when the country was smashed.
Amelia, lady of poverty and no hope,
saint of this earth if ever there
is a saint and if not then you
are what was always instilled in us
as what a saint is, woman in the
retinas of God's eyes for your simple courage
and great accomplishment with no money
and from work that kills young, yet
you still live, Amelia, and here we are.

I came to you the day I
went into the army
      where sardines stuck
to your hands I came and said
goodbye in the fish smell.

You were beautiful, a
beautiful woman and
I yearned to say goodbye
to a mother.

You worked the Sardine Factories
      to feed your children.

No fish contributes
more to the human
race as Herring.

      We sneak death again,
      kill . . . take
      herring from the sea our
      boat circling, the Cannery
      boats lifting the sardines
      aboard into their holds
      through hoses.

A Seine around
fish in moon black.

Draw string of net
pulled to close the
net bottom or the
fish sucked through hose . . .

> To the Cannery as
> soon as fish are
> aboard, Herring
> through a hose removing
> their scales for imitation Pearl
> essence on the Market Place
> and Cosmetics.

IV

Amelia, the fish have less
chance than you had
except your death would
be more subtle, you died
from it, Amelia, died from exhausting
survival, your life wearing
out your life.

> . . . no machine can pack sardines
> like human hands, Amelia . . .

> to feed your children.

Sitting in draughty cold
snipping off dead fish heads and tails
with scissors.

Yet death always a sneak, here

is food to eat but it will decompose
if we do not know that herring who have
just eaten must be allowed to swim it off until
they digest whatever was in them as you catch them . . .
or whatever they were eating avenges them as
bacteria planktonic form . . .

And once caught out of the fresh salt
protecting ocean if the fish are taken
distance of more that four hours they spoil,
Amelia . . . life is death all spoiled.

V

Amelia, did you go north
in the few years of the Winter Fisheries
to Eastport-Lubec, Maine, freezing
nets of two and one half inch mesh
sunk to the bottom in twenty
fathoms of water, fish catch
frozen solid on the market as "boaters."

Amelia, sitting in frigid
cold icy sea water splashing
and wind finding you through
building cracks.

The cooked fish come down
conveyor belts for you to
pick up without breaking them
and put them into cans of
oil or mustard, fast!
You were fast all day
or out of work . . .

        to feed your children.

And to feed your children, bending in
Blueberry fields making your numb
fingers pick fast
to fill up pails quick
without bruising the blueberries
or you'd be out of work!

Vaccinium, that scrub
growing wild on barren uplands
of Maine bearing clustered, mild
sweet tasting fruit either blue
or purple black and coated with
greyish powder . . . Amelia you were
paid not by the time you
spent raking your bony hands blistered
slippery flesh but by the amount
you raked . . . There is no other way
to harvest blueberries other than to
bend over from the waist, tough back,
strong wrists, the strength
put in you by your children to
feed, to pull for, pull
pick through blueberry bushes
with a gentle rocking motion . . .

        to feed your children.

Amelia, how could you love
Maine, the blood blue ocean,
the black green pines and
fresh yellow and green
dandelions with your nose
plowed in the earth or
in the stink of the
dead of the sea.

Although you were no whore
you were as exploited
and paid for piece work . . .

to feed your children.

VI

And into Clam Factories

to feed your children . . .

At night you'd take
hold of one of your hands with the other hand
and grip to squeeze out the pain of
Clam shell tiny cuts so you could sleep . . . to
be able to get up another morning to

feed your children.

And all you ever said anything
about was your sorrow at no time
or opportunity for education to be
accredited a nurse for the bed pans you carried
to feed your children . . . and assist the almost dying
whose saved lives never knew you were ignorant.

VII

In my lost mother boyhood
I stumbled over her kitchen cookies.

Now I am written
where she is in this world.

Her face is now under a spider web.

I have to look hard for
my memory to find it but
her voice is still
that inflection I remember.

       She looks at me with
        mixed emotions at best . . . if
I ever loved her at all then why
have thirty years gone without a
word from me, no note, never
a Christmas card . . .

      Because she
is not the obligation my mother
would be . . .

            I would not have you know, Amelia,
            my years struggling to be my own me
            and not what would please others who
            would be under a head stone just
            when I needed them, just as
            our love affair was coming

And I called out

      "Here I am the way you wanted me" . . . but
they were not there.

VIII

Amelia, Mrs. Brooks of my old childhood, I
have come to you again.

I was suddenly told where
to find you and I broke
New England until here

you and I are again, here
we are both of us in your
little apartment.

We both have died since
we've seen each other.

You speak to me now
and we both feel uncomfortable,
ours is a relationship of wish.

You tell me deaths and
I tell you deaths . . .
They almost killed us both
when they happened but telling
is embarrassing like what
are we talking about!

We have always lived
under the belief
that there is no help!

IX

. . . One of your sons, I remember him, Bob, I
severed Mass with him on altars of
sour wine on early morning air and
bad breath smell from orifice emissions
in the middle of fervent prayers
and closed windows . . . Bob
tripped into an airplane propeller
instead of flying the plane
home for Thanksgiving.

Yet you tell this to me without
even a wince or remorse of

the anguish in your
voice of expression . . .

Because just going through
bringing him up
wore out your tears . . . long ago.
You lived through days you
never thought you'd see
the end of and yet
tomorrow was no relief.

And I do not react
either, death
will finally be my death.

It is strange to think you loved me,
the way you told your
Sister-in-law

        "I just love that boy!"

You would like to love me I
was a boy with no mother and
you had no one either
and often thought of dying and
leaving your children
without a mother . . .

It makes you believe
you love me and
in your old years the
memory of little me running round
may make you believe
you love me.

X

Now in this midnight of
my lost mother boyhood we may
never see each other again.

       A letter appeared telling me
where you were and since I
found myself still alive I
came to you once more . . .

      The sea is in
your voice and my life is
etched in the lines of your face.

If a woman like you wants to
think she loves me, take me
again in your heart in my old childhood.
For soon earth will cover us.

Hydrogen Now

Is that was
isn't is it?
Is that isn't now
is frightening
isn't it?

Blueberry Boy

I only wish I could have it just once more,
you go back and the place looks dull and
small in its mosquito biting green.

I was a Blueberry boy in that childhood,
the sun would flush my freckles out
from where winter hid them in the
sallow pale color of snow and I would
run the meadow for blueberries that
my aunt Madge would turn into muffins
I have longed for down the tripup of manhood.

Just a minute again, on my knees, picking
frantically with expert watered tongue,
ignorant of what lay out of the woods.

In Maine We Own Our Sea

On a tombstone in Thomaston, Maine cemetery
are letters spelling out my ancestor
carved like doughnuts in granite. All the sea
did not get was his name. It was before the
Rockland Breakwater holding ocean undertow
with a stone Judo punch.

In the old days as the boats came in at sunset,
fatigue on the faces of worn out winners
told us the sea had lost. Now the ocean will never win.

We own our sea in Maine. We rode the highest bucking wave
and broke it with the big engines of our power boats
throwing oil in the eyes of the tide.

Now fish fly ice packed to Berkeley, California,
green profit floats down through our pines, and our
graveyard is slow filling in this infancy of earth orbit.

From Five Islands Maine Rocks

The wrinkled sea lined with
near dying experience like faces
of toads, survived as ice
water too cold to perish slips
out to tip over ships and wrestle
the sailors down to its tomb and
I know this land rugged with
the insides to outlast whatever nuclear
springs tomorrow out of its powder-puff.

What I breathe is clear and sharp to
snap my wits again as man
when there was no help but his two gnarled
hands shaping dreams to his own making.

From Five Islands Maine rocks where
Perry-Wrinkles crouch in pools of low tide ocean,
I am myself renewed to kick terror aside and
make a world again where people do not run
but shape a forever instead of our universal end.

Unsafe Survivor

A Fisherman went out without
paying attention. That's th' new-comers! We
allays went to sea runnin' th' boat by

watch-n-compass buoy to buoy like
goin' hand over hand; never heard a' radar!
You look at your watch, go south ten minutes, east

ten minutes to find th' buoy bobbin' on th' water. If
you don't find th' buoy your boat goes down-n-you
drown, maybe, swallowed gone forever. Cemeteries

full of stone spelling Maine lost at sea but
this fisherman was one-a-us, th' new generation! We'd
like him t' be one a' th' new comers, still lazy's lazy-n-

callous 's callous new comers throwin in t'buy a
lobster boat to use like it was their lobster yacht to
just go out on th' treacherous water. Th' new comers

disgust us, they got money f' boats-n-gear but are
unsafe survivors talkin' 'bout "th' ree-ul Maine" to
us. We know th' real Maine and th' horse flies!

When you stay among us as if you are us it will take
a few hundred years before you are us, but in these
scary times one a'them had t'be rescued. He was out

on th' ocean off th' town he come from so he felt safe
but he wasn't. He had his engine off. He tried to start
th' engine but it wouldn't. He puttered, th' wind blown

up and he suddenly didn't know where he was. Death

tossed a ballet of fog over him, water grey in sea-weed
blue white froth smooth. Coast Guard asked him to

anchor so he wouldn't drift. He said he didn't have
an anchor, c'n you imagine on a'us saying that!?
    "Course you do." Coast Guard voice said

and told him where it was down below decks by th' engine
in th' boat. "I forgot about that," he said, then
    "But I've got no anchor rope."

    "Well, You've got plenty of pot warp."
what strings lobster pots together so you toss
them out onto th' sea where they sink like a

jumble of derailed strung together toy freight trains,
traps netted with a hole for lobster to swim into
and through for bait but drop inside the trap caught, so

he tied together enough pot warp to make up length showing
on his depth finder and he dropped anchor but it didn't
catch on anything and wind was driving him further out

to sea. Then Coast Guard asked him why he didn't use
the EPIRB of the geological placement system that
broadcasts to satellites and if you can get picked up

by three satellites then Coast Guard can triangulate the
signals and get your exact location . . . well, our unsafe
survivor had some brains! He shut off his engine now

seeming to know to let the battery recharge
to get power to show Coast Guard light. Now a listening
ham operator called Coast Guard and suggested they

should ask unsafe survivor if he had the EPIRB on deck
or was he trying to broadcast from the cabin . . . hate to

tell you this 'bout one-a-us but sure enough he had it

below. When he brought it up on deck it worked fine and
Coast Guard found him.
    "Where you want to go?" they asked him.
"Wherever you take me is where I'm going," he said.

Garbage Truck

Man built scavenger come
at firing squad time, the
low time of morning
when we most need to be loved
lest we rave our streets screaming
from the piled up truth.
We turn our sleek bellies to balloons
full of canned dead things and lie
wheezing in each other's arms
calling the grave until
it answers.

The End of the World

They have seen the lobster water go dry.
Cold is the empty salt ocean in wake.
The lobster have been scooped out and are gone.
No more do empty baited traps fill.

Greed has drained the sea of its orange fruit.
Now the hard working men who wore themselves out
rising early and ripping the palms of their hands with rope
have time to go bathing like tourists.

Their taut wiry muscles will snag like unwound violins.
And they are dying looking at the ocean with nothing in it to go
after.
The lobsters may be gone in Penobscot forever, certainly
putting out the traps again now will not bring them back.

Out Jim Moore's Window

Out Jim Moore's window,
in the living room of his house in Glen Cove, Maine,
stealing this visit like a dart on a boomerang,
my blue Atlantic boyhood scrutinizes me off
the slip borders of the Penobscot across Strawberry Hill.

See through glass, over Jim's patio back lawn,
tough fading green that light went out of from salt,
the beautiful water of the cove unchanged.

I remember the boy who looked out on that sea water
knowing it would take him to the world,
to blind all this in his accomplishment.

All come back to me here
in the silence of maturity's afternoon.
Things go wrong. We fail.

I am no longer bursting juice skinny youth,
but a man staggered by risks. Yet back across Kittery bridge,
things to do still must be
and I can't come home until they're done.